Cross X Purposes

one granny square, countless possibilities

by Shelley Husband

Copyright © 2025 by Shelley Husband

All rights reserved. No part of this publication may be reproduced or transmitted by any means, electronic, photocopying or otherwise without prior written permission of the author.

ISBN: 978-1-7637215-1-7

Graphic Design & Charts by Michelle Lorimer
Email: hello@michellelorimer.com

Technical Editing by Kelly Lonergan
Email: kelly@hazennainspired.com

Project Photography by Leah Ladson
Website: leahladson.com

Other Photography by Shelley Husband

First edition 2025

Published by Shelley Husband
PO Box 387
Golden Square VIC 3555
Australia

shelleyhusbandcrochet.com

0725

Contents

Welcome to Cross Purposes! | 4

Stitches and Techniques Used in Cross Purposes | 6

Cross Purposes Granny Square Patterns | 12
Cross Purposes One Colour Pattern | 13
Cross Purposes One Colour Pattern Help | 16
Cross Purposes Two Colour Pattern | 25
Cross Purposes Two Colour Pattern Help | 28

Extending the Cross Purposes Pattern | 36

Assembling Your Cross Purposes Project | 41
Border Options | 58

Planning Your Own Cross Purposes Project | 60

Ready to Go Cross Purposes Projects | 70
Giant Granny Square Lap Blanket | 72
Rainbow Cross Purposes Blanket | 75
Cross Purposes Scarf | 79

Cross Purposes Resources | 85

Thank You! | 93

About the Author | 94

Other Books by Shelley Husband | 95

Welcome to Cross Purposes!

So much more than a granny square pattern, Cross Purposes serves many uses, hence the name. I was at "cross purposes" when I was designing it as to what it would become. I could not decide between all the options available to me. So, I decided to try to cover many of the possible purposes for it in one publication.

Within Cross Purposes, you have one granny square pattern and the choice of what to make.

Plan your own project

Cross Purposes comes with help to plan your own project. Work out what you want to make, decide on yarn and how much you will need, and how to choose the hook size. Don't be scared! I am here to step you through the process.

This process is one you can apply to anything. Hence Cross Purposes not really being just a granny square pattern, as you can come back anytime to plan your next project using one or more other granny square patterns.

The knowledge in these pages is transferrable to many other crochet projects, not just in the planning, but the tips and tricks you'll learn along the way to make your crochet sing.

◀ **Scan to download the digital version of Cross Purposes.**

Ready to Go Projects

If choosing your own adventure is too scary and/or you just want to crochet a thing and be told what to get to make it. Well, I've got you.

There are three projects already made with samples and all the yarn needs and instructions to make them ready to go.

How it works

I've structured Cross Purposes as a course. Many parts have worksheets and video accessed via QR codes.

You can skip to the parts you need at any time. If you want to work out how to make your own project, go to the **Planning Your Own Cross Purposes Project** chapter on page 60. If you want to just make a ready to go thing, go to the **Ready to Go Cross Purposes Projects** chapter on page 70.

You'll see the **Cross Purposes Granny Square Patterns** chapter has 2 versions of the pattern. One is if you are using one colour and the other if you are using two colours. Both have a chart and video (with left-handed versions), extra help and round by round photos.

There's a joining chapter - **Assembling Your Cross Purposes Project**, with video. Under this chapter there is the **Border Options** section, with a couple of options to finish your project, depending on what you make.

If you've always been afraid of blocking, well fear no longer! I have stepped out different blocking methods for squares and finished projects.

In short, all the things you need to plan and make your own Cross Purposes projects are right here.

Ok! Let's go!

Welcome to Cross Purposes!

Stitches and Techniques Used in Cross Purposes

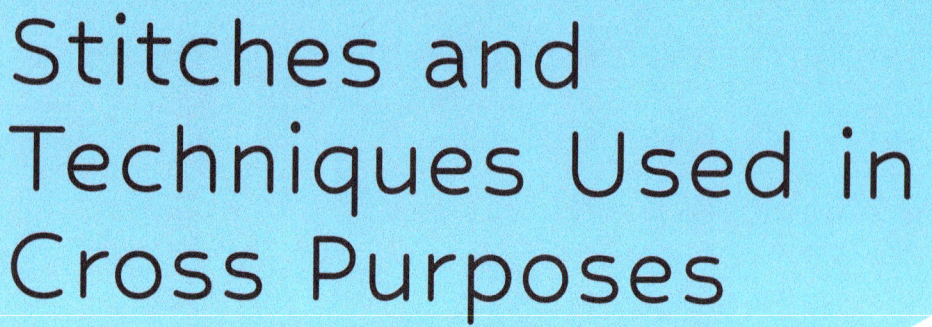

How to work all the stitches and techniques used in the Cross Purposes granny square pattern

 *Slip Stitch*

I know, I know. You know how to do this.

There are nuances though that can help make your work look better.

Such as when joining to a standing stitch, used in the Two Colour Cross Purposes granny square.

The way you make your slip stitch in this case, can make a big difference.

These are examples **(A)** of joining with a slip stitch to a standing stitch, done without being mindful of the process.

And these **(B)** are the same joins with a slip stitch to a standing stitch with some care taken.

Much better, isn't it?

It's all in how you place the yarn over for your slip stitch and the tension when making it.

You make sure your yarn over is sitting under the slip knot and you have firm tension when making the slip stitch **(C)**.

In the video, I show how to slip stitch into:

- a starting chain
- a false stitch
- a standing stitch
- a real stitch

(A)

(B)

(C)

Stitches and Techniques Used in Cross Purposes

 ## *Slip knot*

A slip knot is something you probably do without thinking. It's hard to stop and think about how you make it.

No matter how you make it, there is one important thing to know about slip knots that will affect your work.

It matters which part of the yarn you make your slip knot with.

If you use the part of the yarn leading to your yarn ball, i.e. the working yarn, you pull that strand to tighten it.

If you use the part of the yarn leading to your yarn tail, you pull that strand to tighten it.

Now, in most cases, it does not matter which you do.

If you are always losing your first chain if starting with a length of chains, then chances are you are making your slip knot with the yarn tail.

Some find it useful to make the slip knot with the tail when attaching yarn with a standing stitch, as you can reduce the size of the loop made with your standing stitch.

In the video, I show both ways of making a slip knot, my way. You can make your slip knots however you like.

Stitches and Techniques Used in Cross Purposes

Chain

Yes, I know you know how to chain.

The video explains a little of the mechanics of chaining (and crocheting in general).

How you twist your hook and where on the shaft you work matters. If you are a tight chainer, the video may help alleviate that issue.

Magic circle – optional

I use a magic circle most of the time with my granny squares. But it is optional.

If you don't like it, you can also begin the Cross Purposes granny square in these ways:

- attach yarn to hook with a slip knot, chain 4 and slip stitch into the first chain to make a ring to work into
- attach yarn to hook with a slip knot, chain 1 and work all Round 1 stitches into that 1 chain

The thing to note with a magic circle is that you must weave in your ends well as there is no knot.

The video shows how I make a magic circle.

Double crochet/single crochet (UK/US)

Ah the small stitch - double crochet in UK terms, single crochet in US terms.

This stitch is used for entire rounds in the Cross Purposes granny square as well as for the joining of some rounds.

The video shows how to make the stitch into another stitch and a chain space.

Stitches and Techniques Used in Cross Purposes

Treble crochet/double crochet (UK/US)

The regular old stitch you can probably do in your sleep. A treble crochet in UK terms, called a double crochet in US terms.

Always good to check the technique though, as sometimes folks add an extra step when going from memory.

The video shows how to work the stitch into another stitch and a chain space.

Half double treble crochet/half triple crochet (UK/US)

This stitch may be new to you! It's the half double treble crochet in UK terms and the half triple crochet in US terms.

It's not quite as tall as a double treble/triple (UK/US), and slightly taller than the treble crochet/double crochet (UK/US).

It's easy once you have a go!

The video shows how to work the stitch into a stitch. I show the making the crosses with this stitch in the **One Colour Pattern Help** and **Two Colour Pattern Help** chapters.

False treble crochet/double crochet (UK/US) – optional

While the pattern will say the traditional "ch3 (stch)" at the start of some rounds I make a false stitch instead as chain 3 stands out to me as too different to a regular stitch. If it doesn't bother you, go ahead and chain 3. I also use the same false stitch when replicating a hdtr/htr (UK/US).

The video shows me making a false treble crochet/double crochet (UK/US).

Standing stitch – optional

This is one way you can attach your next colour yarn if making the two colour version.

The video shows attaching with a standing treble crochet/double crochet (UK/US) and a standing double crochet/single crochet (UK/US).

I show making a standing stitch with both ways of making a slip knot, and how to hide the slip knot as you join the round.

Alternative way to start a new colour

Here's an alternative to the standing stitch when you are joining your next colour and the round begins with a tr/dc (UK/US) represented by a ch3 (stch).

This one is good to use when you are working a solid, stitch-in-every-stitch round as you can crochet over the starting end as you go.

The video shows what I do sometimes: attach yarn with a slip stitch and chain, then work a false stitch.

Attaching new yarn mid round when you run out

Sometimes, you may run out of yarn mid round or come across a knot in the yarn.

This is a way to seamlessly continue.

The video shows how to re-join the yarn when making a:

- double crochet/single crochet (UK/US) and
- treble crochet/double crochet (UK/US)

The bonus with this method is you can crochet over the ends as you continue on with the Cross Purposes granny square.

Stitches and Techniques Used in Cross Purposes

Cross Purposes Granny Square Patterns

Cross Purposes
One Colour Pattern

Here you will find the one colour pattern in both UK and US terms. You can download the patterns if you want using the QR codes in the **Cross Purposes Resources** chapter.

If you're a left-hander, head to the **Cross Purposes Resources** chapter to download a version of the pattern with left-handed charts.

Cross Purposes Granny Square Patterns

UK Terms

Begin with mc.

R1: ch3 (stch), 2tr, *ch2, 3tr*, rep from * to * 2x, ch1, join with dc to 3rd ch of stch.
{3 sts on each side; 4 2-ch cnr sps}

R2: dc over joining dc, *dc in next 3 sts**, (dc, ch2, dc) in 2-ch cnr sp*, rep from * to * 2x & * to ** 1x, dc in same sp as first st, ch1, join with dc to first st. {5 sts on each side; 4 2-ch cnr sps}

R3: ch3 (stch), tr over joining dc, *tr in next 5 sts**, (tr, hdtr, tr) in 2-ch cnr sp*, rep from * to * 2x & * to ** 1x, tr in same sp as first sts, join with ss to 3rd ch of stch. {5 sts on each side; 4 3-st cnrs}

R4: dc in same st as ss, *dc in next 7 sts**, (2dc, ch2, dc) in next st*, rep from * to * 2x & * to ** 1x, 2dc in same st as first st, ch1, join with dc to first st. {10 sts on each side; 4 2-ch cnr sps}

R5: ch3 (stch), tr over joining dc, *5x [skip 1 st, hdtr in next st, hdtr in skipped st]**, (2tr, ch2, 2tr) in 2-ch cnr sp*, rep from * to * 2x & * to ** 1x, 2tr in same sp as first sts, ch 1, join with dc to 3rd ch of stch.
{14 sts on each side; 4 2-ch cnr sps}

R6: dc over joining dc, *skip 1 st, dc in next 13 sts**, (dc, ch2, dc) in 2-ch cnr sp*, rep from * to * 2x & * to ** 1x, dc in same sp as first st, ch1, join with dc to first st.
{15 sts on each side; 4 2-ch cnr sps}

R7: ch3 (stch), tr over joining dc, *tr in next 15 sts**, (tr, hdtr, tr) in 2-ch cnr sp*, rep from * to * 2x & * to ** 1x, tr in same sp as first sts, join with ss to 3rd ch of stch.
{15 sts on each side; 4 3-st cnrs}

R8: dc in same st as ss, *skip 1 st, dc in next 16 sts**, (dc, ch2, dc) in next st*, rep from * to * 2x & * to ** 1x, dc in same st as first st, ch2, join with ss to first st. Fasten off.
{18 sts on each side; 4 2-ch cnr sps}

Cross Purposes Granny Square Patterns

US Terms

Begin with mc.

R1: ch3 (stch), 2dc, *ch2, 3dc*, rep from * to * 2x, ch1, join with sc to 3rd ch of stch.
{3 sts on each side; 4 2-ch cnr sps}

R2: sc over joining sc, *sc in next 3 sts**, (sc, ch2, sc) in 2-ch cnr sp*, rep from * to * 2x & * to ** 1x, sc in same sp as first st, ch1, join with sc to first st. {5 sts on each side; 4 2-ch cnr sps}

R3: ch3 (stch), dc over joining sc, *dc in next 5 sts**, (dc, htr, dc) in 2-ch cnr sp*, rep from * to * 2x & * to ** 1x, dc in same sp as first sts, join with ss to 3rd ch of stch.
{5 sts on each side; 4 3-st cnrs}

R4: sc in same st as ss, *sc in next 7 sts**, (2sc, ch2, sc) in next st*, rep from * to * 2x & * to ** 1x, 2sc in same st as first st, ch1, join with sc to first st. {10 sts on each side; 4 2-ch cnr sps}

R5: ch3 (stch), dc over joining sc, *5x [skip 1 st, htr in next st, htr in skipped st]**, (2dc, ch2, 2dc) in 2-ch cnr sp*, rep from * to * 2x & * to ** 1x, 2dc in same sp as first sts, ch 1, join with sc to 3rd ch of stch.
{14 sts on each side; 4 2-ch cnr sps}

R6: sc over joining sc, *skip 1 st, sc in next 13 sts**, (sc, ch2, sc) in 2-ch cnr sp*, rep from * to * 2x & * to ** 1x, sc in same sp as first st, ch1, join with sc to first st.
{15 sts on each side; 4 2-ch cnr sps}

R7: ch3 (stch), dc over joining sc, *dc in next 15 sts**, (dc, htr, dc) in 2-ch cnr sp*, rep from * to * 2x & * to ** 1x, dc in same sp as first sts, join with ss to 3rd ch of stch.
{15 sts on each side; 4 3-st cnrs}

R8: sc in same st as ss, *skip 1 st, sc in next 16 sts**, (sc, ch2, sc) in next st*, rep from * to * 2x & * to ** 1x, sc in same st as first st, ch2, join with ss to first st. Fasten off.
{18 sts on each side; 4 2-ch cnr sps}

Cross Purposes Granny Square Patterns

Cross Purposes
One Colour Pattern Help

Video help

 Scan to watch the Cross Purposes one colour granny square video.

 Scan to watch the Cross Purposes one colour granny square video mirrored for left-handers.

Round 1

Check the **Stitches and Techniques Used in Cross Purposes** chapter if any of the the following is new to you.

You can work the ch3 at the start, or you can work a false stitch instead.

Regardless of which you use, pop a stitch marker in the loop on the right of the third chain (left for left handers) or in the top of your false stitch as soon as you make it. This will help at the end of the round and at the start of Round 2.

 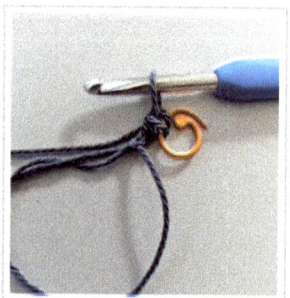

The round ends with ch1 and join with a dc/sc (UK/US). This is an important part of my seamless ways. You will join to where the stitch marker is. Leave the marker in, even after you join the round.

Round 2

The first stitch is worked over the joining stitch.

Cross Purposes Granny Square Patterns

Place a marker in that first st as soon as you make it.

Now, here's where the marker you put in at the start of Round 1 comes in. That shows where to work the first of the three stitches along the side.

You can take the Round 1 marker out now.

After your corners, if the first stitch of the side is obscured, pull the corner stitches to the right (left for left handers) and the "P" of the stitch to work into will appear.

At the end of the round, you need to work a stitch in the same space as the first st:

Now, before you join, pop a scrap of yarn in the gap between your first and last stitches of Round 2.

Cross Purposes Granny Square Patterns

This will help you work Round 3. Leave the stitch marker in the first stitch as you ch1 and join with a dc/sc (UK/US).

Round 3

Same as for Round 1, pop a stitch marker in your third chain or false stitch as soon as you make it.

Work a tr/dc (UK/US) over the joining stitch. The scrap of yarn is in where you need to poke your hook. Leave the scrap of yarn in.

Now work a tr/dc (UK/US) in each of the 5 stitches along the side. The stitch marker from Round 2 will show you where to work the first stitch. Take that marker out.

The corners in this round are three stitches. UK terms: (tr, hdtr, tr), US terms: (dc, htr, dc).

NOTE: if using false stitches, working a false tr/dc (UK/US) is fine at the start

At the end of the round, work a stitch in the same space as the first stitches, where the scrap of yarn is.

Cross Purposes Granny Square Patterns

Round 4

You can take out all stitch markers and scraps of yarn, except the one in your third chain or false stitch of R3.

Before you start, it may help to place a stitch marker in the middle stitch of each 3-stitch corner.

This round is not symmetrical on purpose. We are going from an odd numbered stitch count to an even one.

Start with a stitch in the same stitch as where you worked your slip stitch - ie: in your 3rd ch of the stch or false stitch. Pop a marker in that stitch as soon as you make it.

Now work a stitch in the next 7 sts. The next stitch should be the middle one of the 3-stitch corner.

Cross Purposes Granny Square Patterns

Here's where the asymmetry comes in. The corner is (2 sts, ch2, 1 st).

At the end of the round, you need to work 2 stitches into the same stitch as the first stitch.

Not where the stitch marker is, but where the stitch that marker is in is worked.

Now it's time to pop that scrap of yarn in the gap again before you ch1 and join with a dc/sc (UK/US).

You join to where the marker is. Leave it in.

Round 5

Here's where we work the crosses!

Begin with ch3 or a false stitch and pop a marker in it, then a stitch over the joining stitch, where the scrap of yarn is.

To make the cross shapes along the side, skip one stitch, work a hdtr/htr (UK/US) in the next stitch, then work the same stitch into the one you skipped. The first one into the skipped stitch will be where the marker is. You can take that marker out now.

Be careful when you work your next cross shape. You need to make sure you are skipping a stitch. It can look like the one you used for the first leg of the cross hasn't been used.

You should have 5 crosses on the side and use all 10 stitches of Round 4.

The corners are easy.

Again, if the first stitch of the side after the corner is obscured, pull the corner stitches aside.

At the end of the round, it's time to work 2 stitches into the same space as the first stitches, where the scrap of yarn is.

Cross Purposes Granny Square Patterns

Then, ch1 and join with a stitch to the first one where the marker is. Up to you if you want to put the scrap of yarn in the gap before you join.

Round 6

You should be ok from here on in, as the corners and methods are the same as previous rounds, but I will highlight the differences for you. Keep on using markers and scraps of yarn as you need.

The first stitch of each side is skipped. This gets us back to an odd numbered stitch count.

Round 7

No stitches are skipped, and the corners are three stitch corners, just like in Round 3.

Round 8

This one is just like Round 6, you skip the first stitch of each side, getting us back to an even stitch count.*

***If extending the pattern or using the repeats as a border, in the last Round 8 repeat, don't skip the first stitch of each side.**

Cross Purposes Granny Square Patterns

Cross Purposes
Two Colour Pattern

Here you will find the two colour pattern in both UK and US terms. You can download the patterns if you want using the QR codes in the **Cross Purposes Resources** chapter.

If you're a left-hander, head to the **Cross Purposes Resources** chapter to download a version of the pattern with left-handed charts.

Just a note: this is just one of many ways you can play with colour with the Cross Purposes granny square. Want to do it differently? Go for it.

Cross Purposes Granny Square Patterns

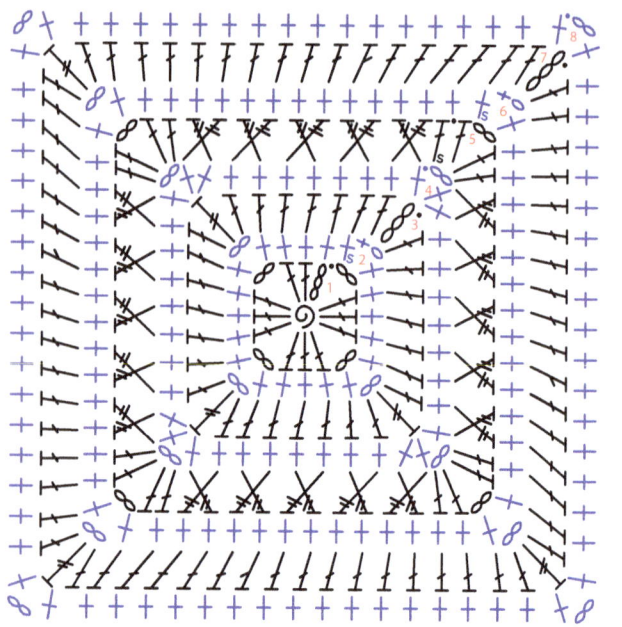

UK Terms

Using Col 2, begin with mc.

R1: ch3 (stch), 2tr, *ch2, 3tr*, rep from * to * 2x, ch2, join with ss to 3rd ch of stch. Fasten off. {3 sts on each side; 4 2-ch cnr sps}

R2: Attach Col 1 with stdg dc in any 2-ch cnr sp, *dc in next 3 sts**, (dc, ch2, dc) in 2-ch cnr sp*, rep from * to * 2x & * to ** 1x, dc in same sp as first st, ch1, join with dc to first st. {5 sts on each side; 4 2-ch cnr sps}

R3: ch3 (stch), tr over joining dc, *tr in next 5 sts**, (tr, hdtr, tr) in 2-ch cnr sp*, rep from * to * 2x & * to ** 1x, tr in same sp as first sts, join with ss to 3rd ch of stch. {5 sts on each side; 4 3-st cnrs}

R4: dc in same st as ss, *dc in next 7 sts**, (2dc, ch2, dc) in next st*, rep from * to * 2x & * to ** 1x, 2dc in same st as first st, ch2, join with ss to first st. Fasten off. {10 sts on each side; 4 2-ch cnr sps}

R5: Attach Col 2 with stdg tr to any 2-ch cnr sp, *5x [skip 1 st, hdtr in next st, hdtr in skipped st]**, (2tr, ch2, 2tr) in 2-ch cnr sp*, rep from * to * 2x & * to ** 1x, (2tr, ch2, tr) in same sp as first st, join with ss to first st. Fasten off. {14 sts on each side; 4 2-ch cnr sps}

R6: Attach Col 1 with stdg dc to any 2-ch cnr sp, *skip 1 st, dc in next 13 sts**, (dc, ch2, dc) in 2-ch cnr sp*, rep from * to * 2x & * to ** 1x, dc in same sp as first st, ch1, join with dc to first st. {15 sts on each side; 4 2-ch cnr sps}

R7: ch3 (stch), tr over joining dc, *tr in next 15 sts**, (tr, hdtr, tr) in 2-ch cnr sp*, rep from * to * 2x & * to ** 1x, tr in same sp as first sts, join with ss to 3rd ch of stch. {15 sts on each side; 4 3-st cnrs}

R8: dc in same st as ss, *skip 1 st, dc in next 16 sts**, (dc, ch2, dc) in next st*, rep from * to * 2x & * to ** 1x, dc in same st as first st, ch2, join with ss to first st. Fasten off. {18 sts on each side; 4 2-ch cnr sps}

US Terms

Using Col 2, begin with mc.

R1: ch3 (stch), 2dc, *ch2, 3dc*, rep from * to * 2x, ch2, join with ss to 3rd ch of stch. Fasten off.
{3 sts on each side; 4 2-ch cnr sps}

R2: Attach Col 1 with stdg sc in any 2-ch cnr sp, *sc in next 3 sts**, (sc, ch2, sc) in 2-ch cnr sp*, rep from * to * 2x & * to ** 1x, sc in same sp as first st, ch1, join with sc to first st.
{5 sts on each side; 4 2-ch cnr sps}

R3: ch3 (stch), dc over joining sc, *dc in next 5 sts**, (dc, htr, dc) in 2-ch cnr sp*, rep from * to * 2x & * to ** 1x, dc in same sp as first sts, join with ss to 3rd ch of stch.
{5 sts on each side; 4 3-st cnrs}

R4: sc in same st as ss, *sc in next 7 sts**, (2sc, ch2, sc) in next st*, rep from * to * 2x & * to ** 1x, 2sc in same st as first st, ch2, join with ss to first st. Fasten off.
{10 sts on each side; 4 2-ch cnr sps}

R5: Attach Col 2 with stdg dc to any 2-ch cnr sp, *5x [skip 1 st, htr in next st, htr in skipped st]**, (2dc, ch2, 2dc) in 2-ch cnr sp*, rep from * to * 2x & * to ** 1x, (2dc, ch2, dc) in same sp as first st, join with ss to first st. Fasten off. {14 sts on each side; 4 2-ch cnr sps}

R6: Attach Col 1 with stdg sc to any 2-ch cnr sp, *skip 1 st, sc in next 13 sts**, (sc, ch2, sc) in 2-ch cnr sp*, rep from * to * 2x & * to ** 1x, sc in same sp as first st, ch1, join with sc to first st.
{15 sts on each side; 4 2-ch cnr sps}

R7: ch3 (stch), dc over joining sc, *dc in next 15 sts**, (dc, htr, dc) in 2-ch cnr sp*, rep from * to * 2x & * to ** 1x, dc in same sp as first sts, join with ss to 3rd ch of stch.
{15 sts on each side; 4 3-st cnrs}

R8: sc in same st as ss, *skip 1 st, sc in next 16 sts**, (sc, ch2, sc) in next st*, rep from * to * 2x & * to ** 1x, sc in same st as first st, ch2, join with ss to first st. Fasten off.
{18 sts on each side; 4 2-ch cnr sps}

Cross Purposes Granny Square Patterns

Cross Purposes
Two Colour Pattern Help

Video help

 Scan to watch the Cross Purposes two colour granny square video.

 Scan to watch the Cross Purposes two colour granny square video mirrored for left-handers.

Round 1 - Feature Colour

Check the **Stitches and Techniques Used in Cross Purposes** chapter if any of the the following is new to you.

You can work the ch3 at the start, or you can work a false stitch instead.

Regardless of which you use, pop a stitch marker in the loop on the right of the third chain (left for left handers) or in the top of your false stitch as soon as you make it. This will help at the end of the round.

The round ends with ch2 and join with a slip stitch. Fasten off. Crochet over the end in the next round.

Cross Purposes Granny Square Patterns

Round 2 - Main Colour

The new colour is attached with a standing stitch to a different corner to where you ended Round 1.

Place a marker in that first st as soon as you make it.

Work a stitch in each of the side stitches and then a corner in the 2-chain corner space.

After your corners, if the first stitch of the side is obscured, pull the corner stitches to the right (left for left handers) and the "P" of the stitch to work into will appear.

At the end of the round, you need to work a stitch in the same space as the first st.

Now, before you join, pop a scrap of yarn in the gap between your first and last stitches of Round 2.

Cross Purposes Granny Square Patterns

This will help you work Round 3. Leave the stitch marker in the first stitch as you ch1 and join with a dc/sc (UK/US).

See my tip about joining to a standing stitch in the slip stitch video or the two colour cross purposes video.

Round 3

Same as for Round 1, pop a stitch marker in your third chain or false stitch as soon as you make it.

Work a tr/dc (UK/US) over the joining stitch. The scrap of yarn is in where you need to poke your hook. Leave the scrap of yarn in.

Now work a tr/dc (UK/US) in each of the 5 stitches along the side, working over the tail from your standing stitch. The stitch marker from Round 2 will show you where to work the first stitch. Take that marker out.

The corners in this round are three stitches. UK terms: (tr, hdtr, tr), US terms: (dc, htr, dc).

NOTE: if using false stitches, working a false tr/dc (UK/US) is fine at the start

Cross Purposes Granny Square Patterns

At the end of the round, work a stitch in the same space as the first stitches, where the scrap of yarn is.

R3

Round 4

You can take out all stitch markers and scraps of yarn, except the one in your third chain or false stitch of R3.

Before you start, it may help to place a stitch marker in the middle stitch of each 3-stitch corner.

This round is not symmetrical on purpose. We are going from an odd numbered stitch count to an even one.

Start with a stitch in the same stitch as where you worked your slip stitch - i.e.: your 3rd ch of the stch or false stitch. Pop a marker in that stitch as soon as you make it.

Cross Purposes Granny Square Patterns

Now work a stitch in the next 7 sts. The next stitch should be the middle one of the 3-stitch corner.

Here's where the asymmetry comes in. The corner is (2 sts, ch2, 1 st).

At the end of the round, you need to work 2 stitches into the same stitch as the first stitch.

Not where the stitch marker is, but where the stitch that marker is in is worked.

Now it's time to ch2 and join with a slip stitch. Fasten off.

Cross Purposes Granny Square Patterns

Round 5

As we are only working one round of this colour, and what happens in the next round, I have you start at a different point in the corner than what you may be used to in my patterns.

Begin with a standing stitch in a different corner to where you ended Round 4 and pop a marker in it.

Here's where we work the crosses!

To make the cross shapes along the side, skip one stitch, work a hdtr/htr (UK/US) in the next stitch, then work the same stitch into the one you skipped.

Be careful when you work your next cross shape. You need to make sure you are skipping a stitch. It can look like the one you used for the first leg of the cross hasn't been used.

You should have 5 crosses on the side and use all 10 stitches of Round 4.

Cross Purposes Granny Square Patterns

The corners are easy.

Again, if the first stitch of the side after the corner is obscured, pull the corner stitches aside.

At the end of the round, here's where we make the corner the same as the others, by working (2 stitches, ch2, 1 stitch) into the same space as the first stitches, then join with a slip stitch to the first stitch and fasten off. You can work over the ends in Round 6.

Round 6

You should be ok from here on in, as the corners and methods are the same as previous rounds, but I will highlight the differences for you. Keep on using markers and scraps of yarn as you need.

You can work over the ends of Round 5 as you go. The first stitch of each side is skipped. This gets us back to an odd numbered stitch count.

Cross Purposes Granny Square Patterns

Round 7

No stitches are skipped, and the corners are three stitch corners, just like in Round 3.

Round 8

This one is just like Round 6, you skip the first stitch of each side, getting us back to an even stitch count.*

If extending the pattern or using the repeats as a border, in the last Round 8 repeat, don't skip the first stitch of each side.

Extending the Cross Purposes Pattern

How to Extend the Cross Purposes Pattern

Once you have made it to the end of Round 8 of the Cross Purposes granny square, you have all the skills you need to keep on going and make the granny square the size you want it to be.

All you need to do is repeat rounds 5 to 8.

It is a simple pattern from here, but because there are slight differences between the rounds, it's easy to mis-remember and get off track.

So, use the Cross Purposes Extension spreadsheet to help stick to the pattern when you extend the Cross Purposes granny square pattern. Have it next to you as you work.

It shows for each round up to 30 repeats of Rounds 5-8:

- the number of crosses you should have,
- the number of stitches along each side,
- what the corners of each round are, and
- whether to skip the first stitch of each side or not.

 ◀ **Download the Extension spreadsheet or find it on page 74.**

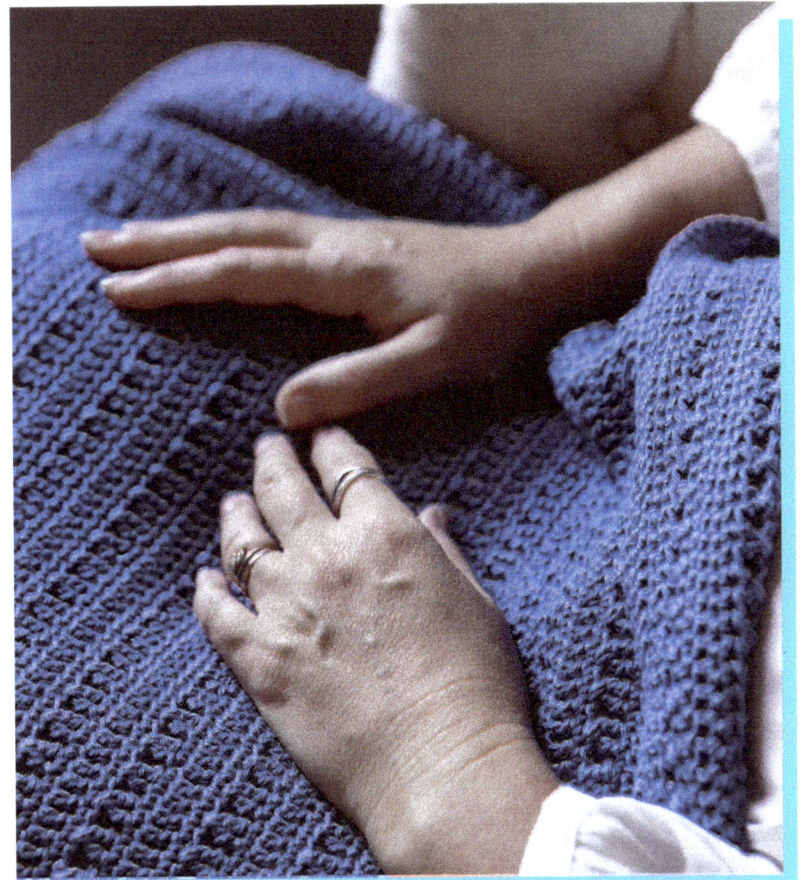

Extending the Cross Purposes Pattern

Fudging when things are a bit off

If you're extending the pattern, it's normal for things to be a bit off now and then.

With this pattern, being off a single stitch is easily dealt with, without the need to count single stitches along long sides.

The crosses round is where you will likely find an oops, usually at the end of a side, where you may find you have three stitches left instead of 2.

Here's where the Cross Purposes Extension spreadsheet mentioned on the previous page comes in handy. Check how many crosses you should have on each side for the repeat you are doing.

If you will be short one cross, work the last cross using the last unused stitch for the first stitch of the cross and place the second stitch of the cross in the second last stitch of the side, even though it was used for the previous cross.

If you will have a stitch left over with the right number of crosses, skip the middle stitch of the three unused to make your last cross.

If you do the corners correctly, (2sts, ch2, 2sts), your stitch counts will be back on track.

Extending the Cross Purposes Pattern

Matching Small and Extended Cross Purposes squares

So, you want to mix and match some different sized Cross Purposes granny squares? Cool. But how exactly do you know how many equals how many repeats when extending.

The short answer is, you'll need to play a bit as you go.

Just know that it's never going to be a perfect to the millimetre size match and have the exact same stitch counts.

So how do you do it?

Start with your small squares. Using the **Project Planner** on page 92, work out how many you want width wise. Make that many squares. Then, start extending. Keep going until the large square roughly matches the size of your small squares but is a bit bigger.

The more you extend, the more small squares you will need to make, which means more joins which will add more width to your strip of small squares.

It's ok if the large square is not exactly the same size, as joining it to the small squares will bring both bits into line. And blocking will finish off the evening out.

Having said all that, here are some examples of actual samples made so you have a rough guide to follow.

Elizabeth's cowl & my joining sample

2 small squares = 1 extended with 2 repeats

Extending the Cross Purposes Pattern

Sarah & Elizabeth's samples

3 small squares = 1 extended with 5 repeats

Scarf made by Adele

5 small squares = 2 extended with 3 repeats

Assembling Your Cross Purposes Project

Dealing with the ends? Blocking? Joining? All the info is here!

Dealing with the ends

Ends are part of crochet. Let's make them just part of the process and not a dreaded task.

The beauty of the Cross Purposes granny square is that even when changing colours, you can mostly work over the ends as you go as I show in the two colour pattern video.

But there are still some ends to deal with.

The video shows how I dealt with the ends from:

- the magic circle centre
- the very last end of a square
- the ends from the cross round if changing colours there.

My hot tip is do them as you go, especially if making lots of squares. Deal with them as you finish each square and you'll have a joyous time once you finish your project.

Video help

◂ **Scan to watch the Weaving in Ends video.**

Joining Cross Purposes granny squares

Yes, there are many ways to join granny squares and you are free to use any method you like.

I am going to share my go-to method used to make the Cross Purposes Rainbow Blanket and the Cross Purposes Scarf/Wrap.

Crochet join

Hold squares right sides together, attach joining yarn with a standing double crochet/single crochet (UK/US) to both 2-chain corner spaces of each square at the same time. Work a double crochet/single crochet (UK/US) into both loops of both squares all the way along, end with a double crochet/single crochet (UK/US) in both 2-chain corner spaces. Fasten off.

How to join a project using all the same sized squares

Layout your squares how you'd like them to be arranged.

Join the squares into strips, then join those strips. When you get to where the squares were joined, use the 2-chain corner space of each square, skipping the join.

Hot tip

Take a photo of your layout to refer to.

Video help

◀ **Scan to watch the Joining video.**

Assembling Your Cross Purposes Project

How to join a project using different sizes squares

Layout your squares how you'd like them to be arranged. Take a photo to refer to.

Look for strips that are the same size as a larger square. Look for small strips that will become the same size as either one larger square or more than one larger square joined. Join the squares into strips, then join those strips. Using stitch markers to hold your strips together can make the job easier.

You may need to do some adjusting for different stitch counts. That is easily done. As many times as needed, use the same stitch on the smaller stitch count strip while using a new stitch on the larger stitch count strip.

The video linked to on the previous page shows:

- joining the same sized squares
- joining strips of the same sized square
- joining strips of different sized squares, adjusting for stitch counts

Assembling Your Cross Purposes Project

Blocking

How to block your Cross Purposes granny squares and projects

Blocking overview

Blocking is an optional thing, but I hope I can convince you that it's worth the time.

The fibre you are using will dictate which blocking method will work best for you.

If using cotton, or a blend of fibres, steam blocking works just fine. I tend to steam block squares as I go and then just the edges of my finished project.

Wool responds best to wet blocking, and I tend to not block as I go and wet block the finished project if using wool.

Tools

I use foam mats - the ones intended for camping flooring - and pins.

These are my blocking pins.

The ball headed ones are all glass headed pins of different lengths. Not on purpose, that's just what I have.

The silver T shaped pins are called T-pins or blocking pins.

The stabby sets of pins in plastic rectangles are blockers.

Assembling Your Cross Purposes Project

This is my back up set I only use when wet blocking if I run out of all of the above pins.

The reason these are backups and just for wet blocking is because they all have plastic heads. Plastic heads and irons don't mix well if you're a clumsy as I am when steam blocking.

Here are some short instructions on steam and wet blocking methods. See the next pages for in depth how to steam and wet block where I show how I blocked each of the Cross Purposes projects.

Steam blocking

Pin out your square and squirt it with steam. I use my iron and hover the iron over the squares for a bit. Once they are cool and dry, the job is done. It takes minutes. Yes, you can use anything that shoots steam.

You don't need anything fancy to block on. A towel works fine, as does pinning directly to an ironing board. I use foam mats intended for temporary flooring.

Wet blocking

Gently wash your project according to the label instructions of your yarn. Usually, that means dunking in tepid water with some kind of wool wash added. Let it soak for 10 to 15 minutes or so, gently squeeze out water then roll between towels to remove more water. Lay flat to dry, pinning edges if needed.

Wet blocking will generally increase the size of your woollen granny squares. The project will determine how much.

For example, my Rainbow blanket grew about a centimetre or two across. The Scarf grew a lot more, because I used a larger hook than normal for the yarn weight. It was the intention it would stretch to show off the lacy pattern.

Assembling Your Cross Purposes Project

Steam blocking step by step

You can use this method for each square as you make it, or to zhoosh up the edges of your finished project.

I use a foam mat, ruled with a one-inch grid to guide my pinning. This allows for in-between measurements as you might find you have with the Cross Purposes pattern. You can also use a towel, an ironing board itself, cardboard if you like.

Blocking squares

Step 1.

Pin out your square to size. Your size is your size. Note what it is for other squares.

Here are three Cross Purposes granny squares, hot off the hook.

Assembling Your Cross Purposes Project

This is stretched too much.

This is not stretched at all.

This is just right.

Here they all are pinned out together so you can see the differences.

Assembling Your Cross Purposes Project

Step 2.

Squirt the square with steam - whatever you have that shoots steam - iron, steamer etc.

If using an iron, hover it over the square for a few seconds.

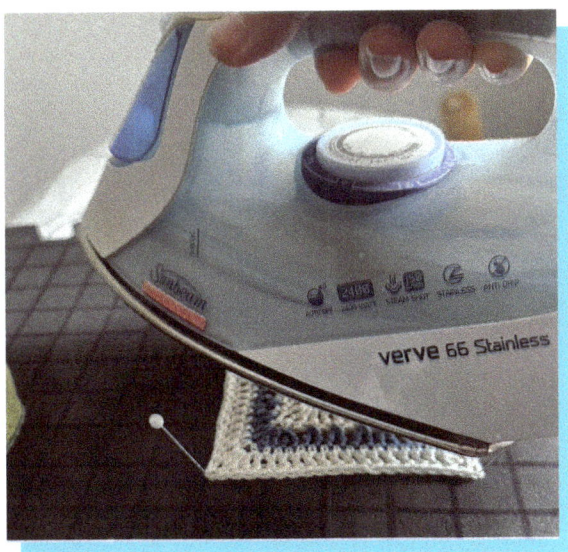

When it's cool and dry (in a few minutes), job done!

Assembling Your Cross Purposes Project

Blocking the edge

If you have lots of blocking mats and the space to do so, lay out your finished project and pin the corners. Place pins along the side as needed. Or if you are limited with space, pin a corner and the edges as far as you can.

Squirt the edge with steam and (hover the iron if you're using one) work along the edge as above.

If doing it in sections, when dry, rotate your project and repeat until all sides and corners are blocked.

Wet Blocking step by step

Wet blocking works best for wool. I wet blocked the Scarf and the Rainbow Blanket and I'll take you through all the steps for each as there were some differences.

With natural wool, you need to be careful as heat and agitation will felt your work. We don't want that. Both the Scarf and the Rainbow Blanket were made with natural wool (i.e. not superwash), so I had to be gentle.

Blocking the Scarf

I added some wool wash to tepid water in my laundry sink, then submerged the scarf, gently squeezing making sure it was all wet and soaked. I left it for 5 to 10 minutes.

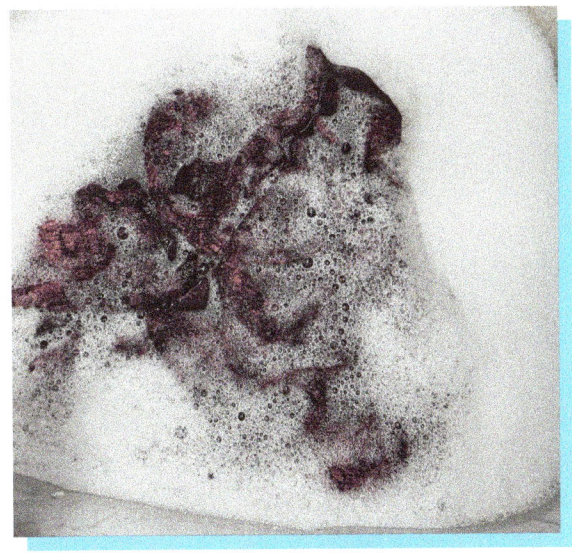

Then, I drained the water and gently squeezed out as much as I could.

Assembling Your Cross Purposes Project

To remove more water, I laid the scarf on a towel, then covered it with another towel.

Rolling the towels and squeezing, by hand and by walking on it, removed a lot more water.

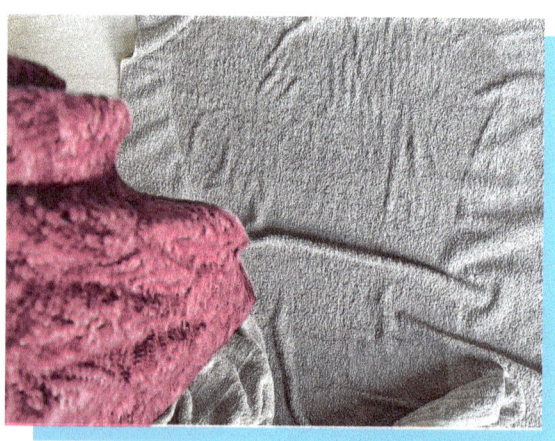

Assembling Your Cross Purposes Project

Then, I laid it out on the blocking mats. As the hook size used is larger than usual for the yarn weight, I knew it this needed some stretching to make it sing. I used the edge of the mats as a guide (luckily the right width for my needs!). I started with the large squares up one end. Making sure the fringe was laid out flat, I pinned the corners and then the join.

I placed pin at each join of small squares to the large squares.

Next, I worked up pulling the small squares at each join to stretch them out before pinning the joins.

Assembling Your Cross Purposes Project

Once I had made my way all the way up the scarf, I pinned the other large squares, again making sure the fringe was lying flat.

The last step was to add pins as needed along the edges to make them straight. No need for pins in the fringes.

Blocking the Rainbow Blanket

I approached this one a little differently. The first steps were the same.

Submerge in a sink with wool wash. Squeeze gently to make sure it was all wet and leave for 5 to 10 minutes.

Drain the water and gently squeeze out as much water as possible. As this was a heavier project, holding it against the side of the sink and squeezing helped.

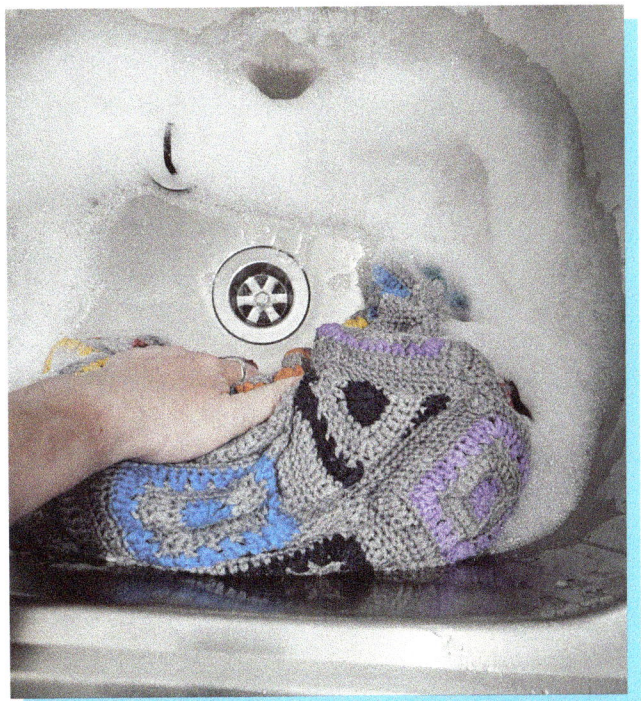

Assembling Your Cross Purposes Project

This is where I changed it up. You could roll it between towels, but I chose to use the spin cycle on my front-loading washing machine. If this would make you nervous, do it in towels. (I am not sure I would do this in a top loader with a central agitator.)

All was well as you can see!

Then, to save my back a bit, I put some blocking mats on the spare bed and spread out the blanket. As it was slightly larger than the mats, I placed folded towels along two edges.

I didn't think this needed a vigorous blocking, so I concentrated on the areas I knew needed it - the joins of the small squares along the inner edge of the border.

I only put a pin in each corner on the outer edge.

Once each project was dry, I removed the pins and called it job done.

Assembling Your Cross Purposes Project

Border Options

Some ideas how to finish your Cross Purposes project.

Option 1 - one colour

The simplest border is using Rounds 6 to 8 of the Cross Purposes granny square in the one colour. In Round 6, make a stitch in each stitch, 2-chain corner space and join.

I could have done this with the Rainbow Blanket version, using the grey colour.

I have done a small sample to show you what that looks like.

When using R8 as the last round of a border, don't skip the first stitch of each side. We skipped the stitch to keep the stitch counts correct for the pattern. As this will be the last round, we don't need to worry about what comes next.

Option 2 - two or more colours

This one is a larger border and can be really big if you want it, as shown in the Rainbow Blanket.

I started with a round of double crochet/single crochet (UK/US) making a stitch in each stitch, 2-chain corner space and join.

Use Rounds 5-8 with round 5 being made in a colour and 6-8 in the neutral.

I made this repeat 7 times with all the colours used in the blanket.

When using R8 as the last round of a border, don't skip the first stitch of each side. We skipped the stitch to keep the stitch counts correct for the pattern. As this will be the last round, we don't need to worry about what comes next.

Assembling Your Cross Purposes Project

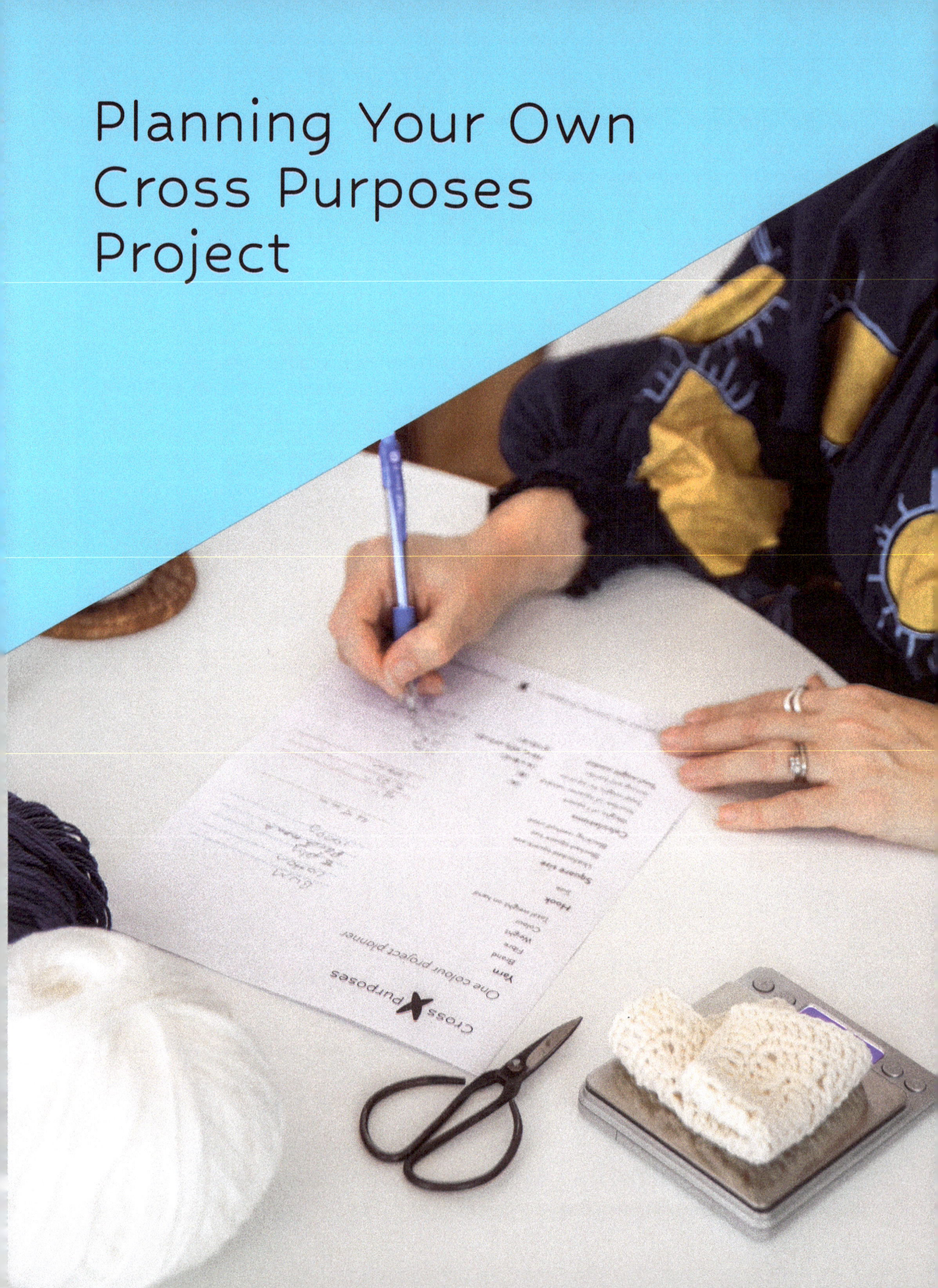

Planning Your Own Cross Purposes Project

Decide What To Make

You could make

Granny squares can be used to make oh so many things!

Here are a few ideas for you:

- a blanket - small, medium, big, square, rectangular - the choice is yours,
- a cushion - or cover - or a panel to sew on a ready-made cushion,
- a cowl - double-wrap length or snug single loop length,
- a scarf - super long and thin, or wide and shawl style, anything in-between, or
- whatever else you can think of.

So have a think. What would suit your personal needs right now?

Things to consider:

- Time available - how many WIPs do you have on the go? Are you working a lot? Family commitments?
- Are you planning to use your stash? How much you have on hand will influence what you can make.
- Need/want to shop? Well, your budget may impact what you do.
- Are you making a gift for someone? What would they appreciate/use?

 ◀ Scan to download the Brainstorming worksheet, or find it on page 89. Jot down some ideas. You can have a few possible options. Sit with them for a bit before you decide.

Planning Your Own Cross Purposes Project

Yarn and Hook Choices

How much yarn will you need? And what hook size will you use?

What yarn will you use? How many colours? What hook size? How much yarn? Let's work it all out.

Yarn choice

Stash dive? Shopping? Up to you of course!

If you're stash diving, you can jump right into the planning. If not, and you don't have the yarn you want to use for your project, well you need to:

1. Test out the pattern with something similar you have on hand (needs to be approximately the same metres per gram as your intended yarn), or
2. source a little bit, if you're not wanting to buy loads just yet, or
3. use my yarn calculations for three yarn weights as a guide.

   - 4 ply/sock/fingering: 8 grams of BWM 3.35 metres per gram
   - 8 ply/DK/light worsted:13 grams of BWM 2.43 metres per gram
   - 10 ply/aran/worsted: 18 grams of BWM 1.8 metres per gram

Cross Purposes is great for using up bits and bobs of stash. If you have loads, well, you can probably just start making and all will be well. But if your stash is not so big, you'll need to work things out.

Sarah made these samples for me using left-over bits of sock yarns along with a neutral.

Maybe you have lots of small amounts of yarn in many colours too. If so, you may only need to source the neutral yarn if you like this idea. Or you may have some in your stash.

If the yarn is the same weight and the same fibre, all will be well. You don't want to mix fibres though - eg superwash with non-superwash, or cotton and wool, as they will wash and wear differently.

Now, the amount you will need, stash diving or not, is going to depend on what you are making. To kick off the planning, the best, most accurate way forward is to make a sample square with your yarn of choice, if possible.

Planning Your Own Cross Purposes Project

One Colour

If you're planning on only using one colour, easy stuff! Make a Cross Purposes square and weigh it - before you weave in the ends and trim them. Use the **One Colour Project Planner** on page 90 or download it and note this info:

- yarn
- hook you used*
- weight of one square before ends are done
- size of the square unblocked**
- size of the square blocked
- blocking method used

> *hook you used. Start with the usual hook size for the yarn you're using. If you don't like the result, try larger or smaller hooks. It's all about what you like the look and feel of, not matching what I made.

> ** yes, I want you to block your sample. Go back to the Blocking chapter for help.

I made these samples using a 4 mm, 4.5 mm, 5 mm and 6 mm hook. In the end, I liked the look and feel of the square with the 5 mm hook.

We'll come back to the One Colour Project Planner soon.

◂ **Scan to download the One Colour Project Planner or find it on page 90.**

Planning Your Own Cross Purposes Project

Two Colour

If you want to use colour per the two colour pattern, then you need to do a bit more work.

It may pay to make a one colour square in a few hook sizes before you start working out the two colour yarn needs. (See the previous page if you skimmed the one colour bit).

Once you are happy with your yarn and hook combination, use the **Two Colour Project Planner** on page 91 or download it, weigh your yarns and make a Two Colour Cross Purposes square, noting:

- yarn info
- hook size
- weigh the 2 yarns you plan to use before you make a sample. Weigh the leftover yarn after you make your square. Note these weights and work out the amount used.
- size of the square unblocked
- size of the square blocked
- blocking method used

 ◂ **Scan to download the Two Colour Project Planner or find it on page 91.**

Okay, so now comes some more planning, regardless of one or two colours, stash diving or not.

Planning Your Own Cross Purposes Project

Plan your layout

Now it's decision time. You need to know what you want to make for this part.

Once you know, use the **Layout Planner** on page 92 or download it.

Note the size of your Cross Purposes square and map out the dimensions of your project.

One square on the planner = one Cross Purposes granny square, not extended.

Let's run through some examples.

1. Lap blanket

I want my blanket to be about 50 inches square. One square in my chosen yarn is about 4.5 inches.

So, I'd colour in a 10 x 10 grid, which will give me a panel about 45 x 45 inches. Adding a simple border as in the Border options section, will make it up to about 50 inches.
10 x 10 = 100 squares.

◄ **Scan to download the Layout Planner or find it on page 92.**

Planning Your Own Cross Purposes Project

2. Cowl

I want my cowl to be snug around my neck, but easy to slide over my head. Using a tape measure, for me that means it needs to be about 26 inches around. And I like it scrunched up so about 9 inches wide.

If my sample square is about 4.5 inches, I'd colour in rectangle 2 squares wide and 6 deep, giving me a cowl 9 x 27 inches. 2 x 6 = 12 squares. I'd do a simple round of dc/sc (UK/US) on each edge, so not much needed edging/border wise.

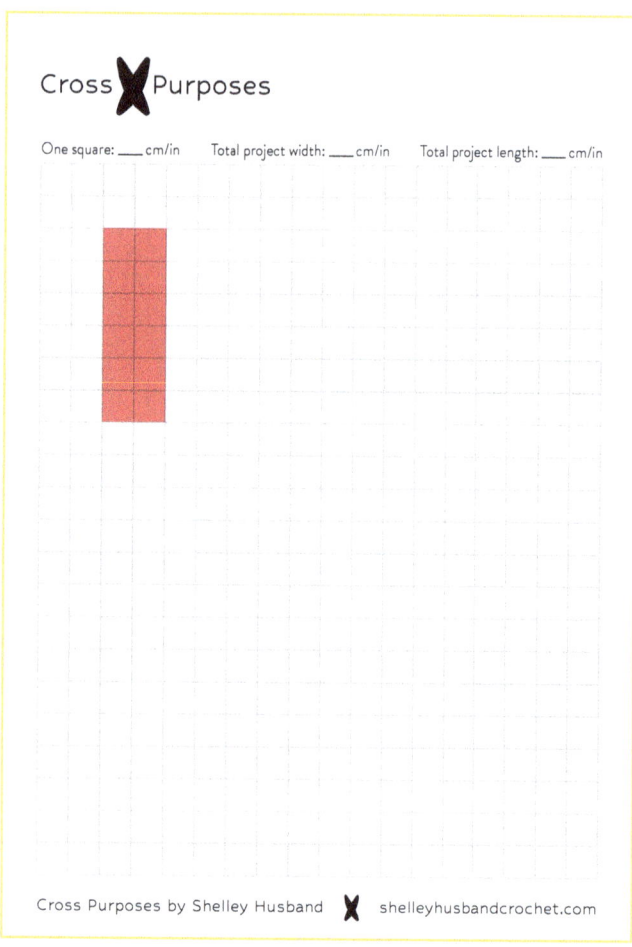

Once you know how many squares you need, you can go back to your One or Two Colour Project Planner and fill in the rest to work out your yarn needs.

Here are sample calculations for the lap blanket examples in one and two colours.

One colour

Fill in the bottom section with the number of squares you need and follow the calculations on the sheet.

Calculations

Weight of 1 square	(A)	10.25g
Number of squares needed	(B)	100
Total weight for squares	(A x B = C)	10.25 x 100 = 1025g (1.025kg)
Joining and border	(10 to 20% of C = D)	15% of 1025g = 153.75g
Total weight needed	(C + D = E)	1025 + 153.75 = 1178.75 g (round up to 1.2 kg)

Two colour

Fill in the bottom section with the number of squares you need and follow the calculations on the sheet.

Calculations

MC weight before making	(A)	50 g
MC weight after making	(B)	42.2 g
FC weight before making	(D)	30 g
FC weight after making	(E)	26.5 g
MC needed for 1 square	(A - B = C)	7.8 g
FC needed for 1 square	(D - E = F)	3.5 g
Number of squares needed	(G)	100
MC Total weight for squares	(C x G = H)	7.8 x 100 = 780 g
FC Total weight needed	(F x G = I)	3.5 x 100 = 350 g
MC Joining and border	(10 to 20% of H = J)	117 g
Total MC weight needed	(H + J = K)	780 + 117 = 897 g (round up to 950 g)

Planning Your Own Cross Purposes Project

Extending Cross Purposes granny square pattern

If you're planning on extending the pattern, either sometimes or the same amount for each square, you can still use the un-extended pattern as a guide to work out your yarn needs.

Say you wanted to make large squares the same size as three small squares. That's a 3 x 3 block on the grid. The yarn needs to make that one large square will be approximately the same as 9 small squares.

So, when planning your yarn needs, regardless of your plans to extend, use the small blocks as your guide. As long as the overall width x depth dimensions are the same, all will be well.

To help you keep on track when extending the Cross Purposes granny square, use the **Extending Cross Purposes** spreadsheet on page 88.

Choosing colours

Now this is not something I can choose for you. Colour preferences are a very individual matter. What I can do is show you some examples and give you some ideas.

If you're making for someone else, check in with them to ask what they're into. They may have told you once long ago that bright pink was their vibe, but they may now prefer soft grey.

If making for yourself, a quick glance at your wardrobe or yarn stash will show you where your preferences lie.

Elizabeth made some samples for me that really show how you can go classic or let your colour-burst love shine.

I love the idea of a bold colour with a neutral like the large red and cream version.

This is the same concept but with a bolder contrast - how cool does the rainbow yarn look in the charcoal?

Or, as shown in the second image to the right made by Sarah, lots of random colours with the one neutral.

You can go with a more neutral vibe all over with 2 similar colours like the example at the bottom of this page, still contrasting but in the same colour.

In the end, this one is down to you.

Other Options

I have detailed things for either one or two colours in all the lessons here, but that my no means limits you to doing either of those options. You can use a different colour each round, three colours in each square, make each square a different colour. There really are so many options!

Planning Your Own Cross Purposes Project

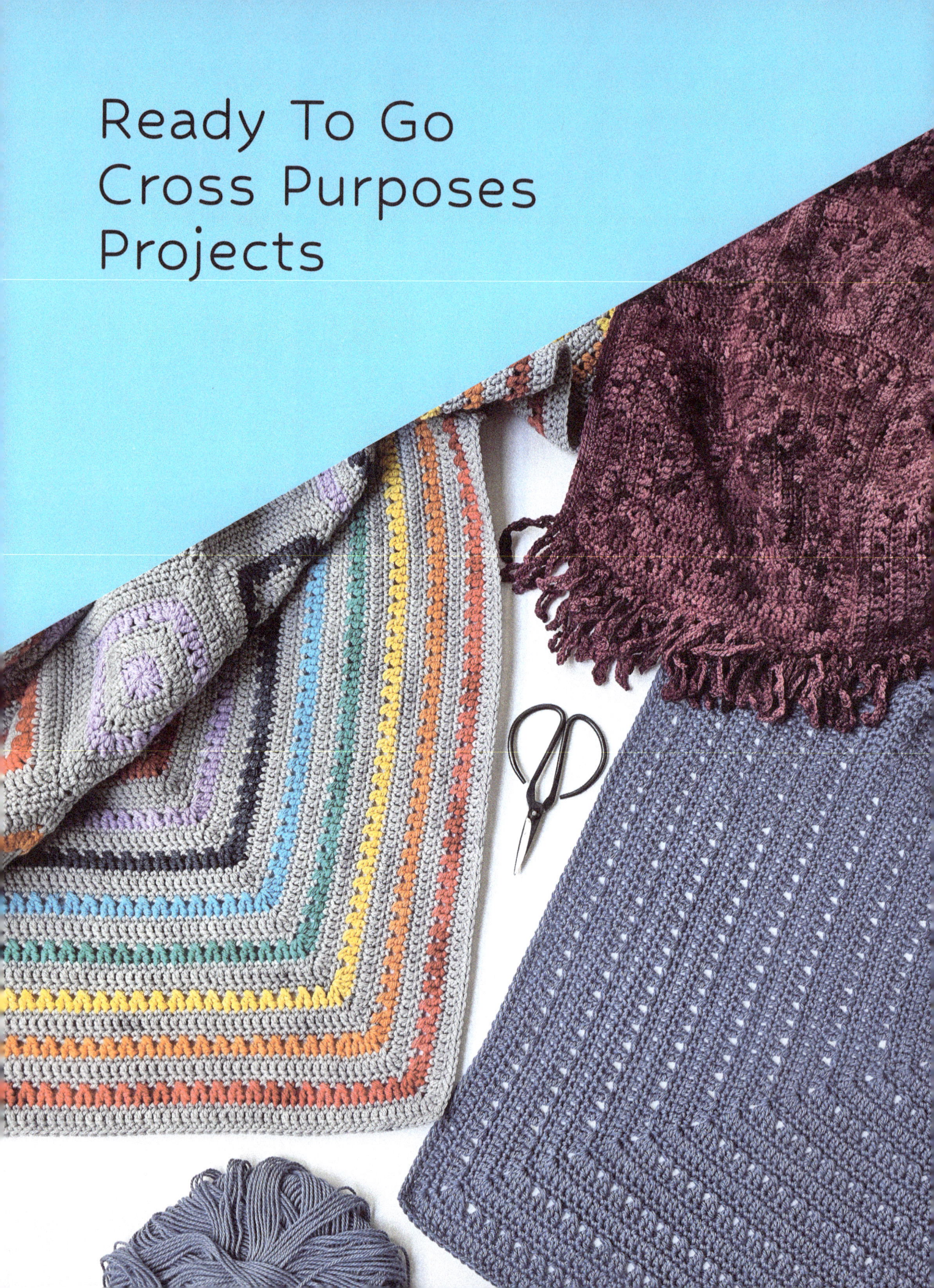

Ready To Go Cross Purposes Projects

Just want to make something,
no planning needed?
I've got you.

Top left: Giant Granny Square Lap Blanket

Top right: Rainbow Blanket

Left: Cross Purposes Scarf

Giant Granny Square Lap Blanket

You can use any yarn and hook you like, but bear in mind that changing the yarn and hook may mean your size and amount yarn needed will be different.

It is a very flexible project though, so don't worry too much about it. If your yarn has a similar metres/gram ratio and you have a size after Round 8 of about 12.5 cm/ 5 in, all will be well.

Check out the **Planning Your Own Cross Purposes Project** chapter if you want to make any changes from my project, e.g. making it bigger or changing the yarn and/or hook size.

Refer to the **Stitches and Techniques Used in Cross Purposes** chapter for help on how to continue when you run out of yarn mid round.

Yarn

Bendigo Woollen Mills 8 ply cotton

- 4 balls (770 grams used)
- 485 metres per 200 gram ball (2.425 metres per gram)

Colour

- Smoky Blue

Hook

- 4.5 mm

Size

- 120 cm x 120 cm/47 in x 47 in
- Gauge check: 14 cm/5.5 in at the end of Round 8.

Make

Make the **Cross Purposes One Colour Granny Square Pattern** on pages 14 & 15, repeating Rounds 5-8 18 times. Use the table on the next page to keep track.

In the last round of the project, don't skip the first stitch of each side. End the last Round 8 repeat with ch2, join with ss to first st at the end. Fasten off.

Video help

Scan to watch the Cross Purposes one colour granny square video.

Scan to watch the Cross Purposes granny square video mirrored for left-handers.

To extend:

- End R8 with: ch1, join with dc/sc to first st.
- Repeat Rounds 5 to 8 18 times.
- Stitch count will increase by 8 each repeat.
- Don't skip the first st of each side in the last R8 repeat.

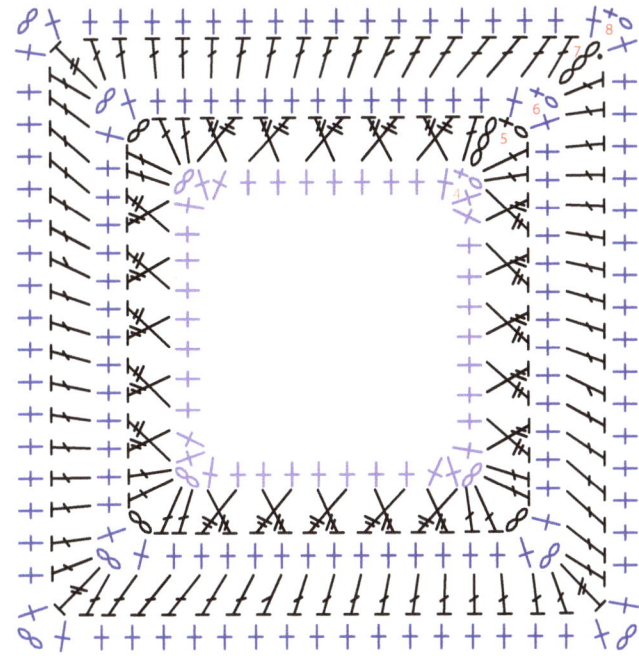

Ready To Go Cross Purposes Projects

Repeat	Round	Side st count	Corners	Skip first st	Crosses	✓
	1	3	2-ch			
	2	5	2-ch	N		
	3	5	3-st	N		
	4	10	2-ch	N		
	5	14	2-ch		5	
	6	15	2-ch	Y		
	7	15	3-st	N		
	8	18	2-ch	Y		
Repeat 1	9	22	2-ch		9	
	10	23	2-ch	Y		
	11	23	3-st	N		
	12	26	2-ch	Y		
Repeat 2	13	30	2-ch		13	
	14	31	2-ch	Y		
	15	31	3-st	N		
	16	34	2-ch	Y		
Repeat 3	17	38	2-ch		17	
	18	39	2-ch	Y		
	19	39	3-st	N		
	20	42	2-ch	Y		
Repeat 4	21	46	2-ch		21	
	22	47	2-ch	Y		
	23	47	3-st	N		
	24	50	2-ch	Y		
Repeat 5	25	54	2-ch		25	
	26	55	2-ch	Y		
	27	55	3-st	N		
	28	58	2-ch	Y		
Repeat 6	29	62	2-ch		29	
	30	63	2-ch	Y		
	31	63	3-st	N		
	32	66	2-ch	Y		
Repeat 7	33	70	2-ch		33	
	34	71	2-ch	Y		
	35	71	3-st	N		
	36	74	2-ch	Y		
Repeat 8	37	78	2-ch		37	
	38	79	2-ch	Y		
	39	79	3-st	N		
	40	82	2-ch	Y		
Repeat 9	41	86	2-ch		41	
	42	87	2-ch	Y		
	43	87	3-st	N		
	44	90	2-ch	Y		
Repeat 10	45	94	2-ch		45	
	46	95	2-ch	Y		
	47	95	3-st	N		
	48	98	2-ch	Y		
Repeat 11	49	102	2-ch		49	
	50	103	2-ch	Y		
	51	103	3-st	N		
	52	106	2-ch	Y		
Repeat 12	53	110	2-ch		53	
	54	111	2-ch	Y		
	55	111	3-st	N		
	56	114	2-ch	Y		
Repeat 13	57	118	2-ch		57	
	58	119	2-ch	Y		
	59	119	3-st	N		
	60	122	2-ch	Y		
Repeat 14	61	126	2-ch		61	
	62	127	2-ch	Y		
	63	127	3-st	N		
	64	130	2-ch	Y		
Repeat 15	65	134	2-ch		65	
	66	135	2-ch	Y		
	67	135	3-st	N		
	68	138	2-ch	Y		
Repeat 16	69	142	2-ch		69	
	70	143	2-ch	Y		
	71	143	3-st	N		
	72	146	2-ch	Y		
Repeat 17	73	150	2-ch		73	
	74	151	2-ch	Y		
	75	151	3-st	N		
	76	154	2-ch	Y		
Repeat 18	77	158	2-ch		77	
	78	159	2-ch	Y		
	79	159	3-st	N		
	80*	163	2-ch	N		

Ready To Go Cross Purposes Projects

Rainbow Cross Purposes Blanket

You can use any yarn and hook you like, but bear in mind that changing the yarn and hook may mean your size and yarn used will be different.

It is a very flexible project though, so don't worry too much about it. If your yarn has a similar metres/gram ratio and one Cross Purposes square is a similar size to me (about 14 cm /5.5 in steam blocked) all will be well.

Check out the **Planning Your Own Cross Purposes Project** chapter if you want to make any changes from my project, e.g. making it bigger or changing the yarn and/or hook size.

Refer to the **Stitches and Techniques Used in Cross Purposes** chapter for help on how to change colours with a standing stitch.

Ready To Go Cross Purposes Projects

Yarn

Bellevue Park 8 ply Wool

- Hand Dyed Hanks
- 238 metres per 100 g skein (2.38 metres per gram)

Colours

- Galvanised Iron (grey), 8 skeins (790 grams used)
- 1 skein each (60 grams of each used approximately) of:
    - Bottlebrush (red)
    - Pumpkin (orange)
    - Canola (yellow)
    - Sea Green (green)
    - Bubblegum (blue)
    - Petrol (indigo)
    - Jacaranda (violet)

Hook

- 4.5 mm

Size

- 135 x 135 cm/53 x 53 in
- Gauge check: 1 square = 14 cm/5.5 in

Make

Make the **Cross Purposes Two Colour Granny Square Pattern** on pages 26 & 27, 7 times with each colour. Use the table to keep track.

Colour	Squares made						
Red							
Orange							
Yellow							
Green							
Blue							
Indigo							
Violet							

Join

R	O	Y	G	B	I	V
V	R	O	Y	G	B	I
I	V	R	O	Y	G	B
B	I	V	R	O	Y	G
G	B	I	V	R	O	Y
Y	G	B	I	V	R	O
O	Y	G	B	I	V	R

Schematic

Referring to the schematic for the order, join into seven strips then join those strips using the following join:

UK Terms

Hold squares right sides together, attach joining yarn with a standing double crochet to both 2-chain corner spaces of each square at the same time. Work a double crochet into both loops of both squares all the way along, end with a double crochet in both 2-chain corner spaces. Fasten off.

US Terms

Hold squares right sides together, attach joining yarn with a standing single crochet to both 2-chain corner spaces of each square at the same time. Work a single crochet into both loops of both squares all the way along, end with a single crochet in both 2-chain corner spaces. Fasten off.

When joining the strips, when you get to where the squares were joined, use the 2-chain corner space of each square, skipping the join.

Border

UK Terms

Round 1

Attach Grey with a stdg dc to any 2-ch cnr sp, *dc in each (st, 2-ch sp & join) along side**, (dc, ch2, dc) in 2-ch cnr sp*, rep from * to * 2x & * to ** 1x, dc in same sp as first st, ch1, join with dc to first st.
{146 sts on each side; 4 2-ch cnr sps}

US Terms

Round 1

Attach Grey with a stdg sc to any 2-ch cnr sp, *sc in each (st, 2-ch sp & join) along side**, (sc, ch2, sc) in 2-ch cnr sp, rep from * to * 2x & * to ** 1x, sc in same sp as first st, ch1, join with sc to first st.
{146 sts on each side; 4 2-ch cnr sps}

Remaining rounds

Beginning with Violet, repeat Rounds 5-8 of the Cross Purposes Two Colour pattern. Progress in reverse order through the rainbow for the Round 5 repeats, ending with Red before the last repeat of Rounds 6-8 in Grey. In the last Round 8 repeat, don't skip the first stitch of the side and end with ch2, join with a slip stitch to first st. Fasten off.

Number of crosses in each coloured R5 repeat	
Violet	73
Indigo	77
Blue	81
Green	85
Yellow	89
Orange	93
Red	97

Video help

Scan to watch the Cross Purposes two colour granny square video.

Scan to watch the Cross Purposes two colour granny square video mirrored for left-handers.

Cross Purposes Scarf

You can use any yarn and hook you like, but bear in mind that changing the yarn and hook may mean your size and yarn used will be different.

It is a very flexible project though, so don't worry too much about it. If your yarn has a similar metres/gram ratio and one Cross Purposes square is a similar size to me (about 10 cm (4 in) unblocked/12 cm (4.75 in) wet blocked) all will be well.

Check out the **Planning Your Own Cross Purposes Project** chapter if you want to make any changes from my project, e.g. making it bigger or changing the yarn and/or hook size.

Refer to the **Extending the Cross Purposes Pattern** chapter for help on how to extend the Cross Purposes granny square pattern.

Ready To Go Cross Purposes Projects

Yarn

Bellevue Park 4 ply Wool

- Hand Dyed Hanks
- 4 skeins (352 grams used)
- 476 metres per 100 gram skein (4.76 metres per gram)

Colour

- Gooseberry Jam

Hook

- 4 mm

Size

- 56 cm wide x 180 cm long (no fringe), 200 cm (inc. fringe)/22 in wide x 71 in long (no fringe) 79 in (inc. fringe)
- Gauge check: 10 cm/4.5 in unblocked 12.5 cm/5 in wet blocked

Video help

 Scan to watch the Cross Purposes one colour granny square video.

 Scan to watch the Cross Purposes one colour granny square video mirrored for left-handers.

Make

Make 50 Cross Purposes Granny Squares up to Round 8.

The **Cross Purposes One Colour Granny Square Pattern** is on pages 14 & 15.

Make 4 Cross Purposes Granny Squares, repeating Rounds 5-8 3 times. End the last Round 8 repeat with ch2, join with ss to first st at the end. Fasten off.

Use the table below to mark off your squares as you make them. Use the chart on the following page to keep track of the round repeats for the four extended squares.

Granny Squares	Number made			
Cross Purposes				
Large Cross Purposes				

Ready To Go Cross Purposes Projects

To extend:

- End R8 with: ch1, join with dc/sc to first st.
- Repeat Rounds 5 to 8 3 times.
- Stitch count will increase by 8 each repeat.
- End the last repeat R8 with ch2, ss join.

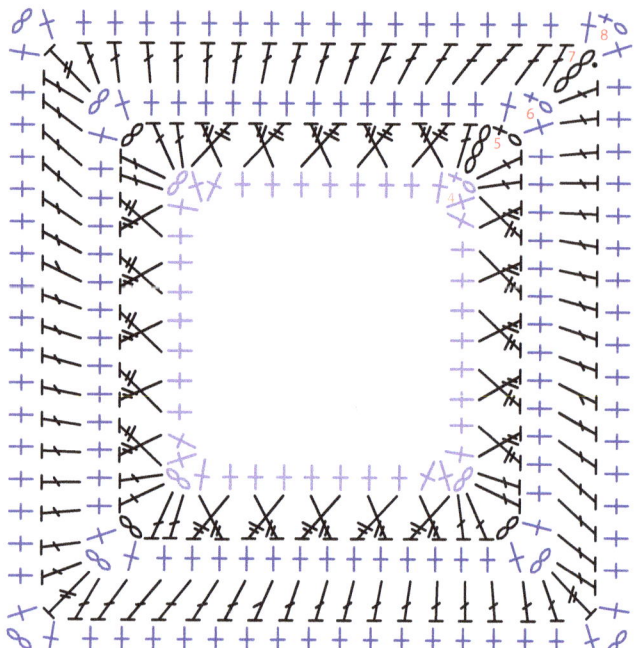

Repeat	Round	Side st count	Corners	Skip first st	Crosses	✓
	1	3	2-ch			
	2	5	2-ch	N		
	3	5	3-st	N		
	4	10	2-ch	N		
	5	14	2-ch		5	
	6	15	2-ch	Y		
	7	15	3-st	N		
	8	18	2-ch	Y		
Repeat 1	9	22	2-ch		9	
	10	23	2-ch	Y		
	11	23	3-st	N		
	12	26	2-ch	Y		
Repeat 2	13	30	2-ch		13	
	14	31	2-ch	Y		
	15	31	3-st	N		
	16	34	2-ch	Y		
Repeat 3	17	38	2-ch		17	
	18	39	2-ch	Y		
	19	39	3-st	N		
	20	42	2-ch	Y		

Ready To Go Cross Purposes Projects

Join

Referring to the schematic, join into strips then join those strips using the following join:

UK Terms

Hold squares right sides together, attach joining yarn with a standing double crochet to both 2-chain corner spaces of each square at the same time. Work a double crochet into both loops of both squares all the way along, end with a double crochet in both 2-chain corner spaces. Fasten off.

US Terms

Hold squares right sides together, attach joining yarn with a standing single crochet to both 2-chain corner spaces of each square at the same time. Work a single crochet into both loops of both squares all the way along, end with a single crochet in both 2-chain corner spaces. Fasten off.

When joining the strips, when you get to where the squares were joined, use the 2-chain corner space of each square, skipping the join.

Schematic

Ready To Go Cross Purposes Projects

Edging/fringe pattern

UK Terms

chfr: ch18, dc in 4th ch from hook, 2x [ch6, skip 5 ch, dc in next ch], ch2

R1: Attach with stdg dc to any 2-ch cnr sp before a long edge, *dc in each (st, 2-ch sp & join) along edge**, (dc, ch2, dc) in 2-ch cnr sp*, rep from * to * 2x & * to ** 1x, dc in same sp as first st, ch1, join with dc to first st.

R2: dc over joining dc, *dc in blo of each st along side, dc in 2-ch cnr sp, chfr, 44x [dc in next st, chfr, skip 1 st], dc in next st, chfr*, dc in 2-ch cnr sp, rep from * to * 1x, join with ss to first st. Fasten off.

US Terms

chfr: ch18, sc in 4th ch from hook, 2x [ch6, skip 5 ch, sc in next ch], ch2

R1: Attach with stdg sc to any 2-ch cnr sp before a long edge, *sc in each (st, 2-ch sp & join) along edge**, (sc, ch2, sc) in 2-ch cnr sp*, rep from * to * 2x & * to ** 1x, sc in same sp as first st, ch1, join with sc to first st.

R2: sc over joining sc, *sc in blo of each st along side, sc in 2-ch cnr sp, chfr, 44x [sc in next st, chfr, skip 1 st], sc in next st, chfr*, sc in 2-ch cnr sp, rep from * to * 1x, join with ss to first st. Fasten off.

Cross Purposes Resources

Glossary

Abbreviations

cnr	corner	
R	round	
rep	repeat	
sp/s	space/s	
st/s	stitch/es	
stch	starting chain	Used in place of the first st in a round. Is included in stitch count.
yo	yarn over	Wrap yarn over hook from back to front.

Stitches UK/US

·	ss	slip stitch	Insert hook into st or sp indicated, yo and pull through st or sp and loop on hook.
o	ch	chain	Yarn over, pull through loop on hook.
+	dc/sc	double crochet/ single crochet	Insert hook into st or sp indicated, yo, pull loop to front, yo, pull through both loops on hook.
┬	tr/dc	treble crochet/ double crochet	Wrap yarn around hook, insert hook into st or sp indicated, yo, pull loop to front (3 loops on hook), 2x [yo, pull through 2 loops on hook].
┬	hdtr/htr	half double treble crochet/half triple crochet	Wrap yarn around hook twice, insert hook into st or sp indicated, yo, pull loop to front (4 loops on hook), yo, pull through 2 loops (3 loops on hook), yo, pull through all 3 loops on hook.

Techniques

↻	mc	magic circle	Method used to begin a square. Wrap yarn around a few fingers, forming a loop, insert your hook into the centre and pull the working yarn through, ch1 to secure. Work R1 sts into the ring, pull the tail to close the ring once all sts have been made and secure by weaving the end in well.

Downloads & Worksheets

 ◄ Download the Extension Spreadsheet

 ◄ Download the Brainstorming Worksheet

 ◄ Download the One Colour Project Planner

 ◄ Download the Two Colour Project Planner

 ◄ Download the Layout Planner

 ◄ Download the Glossary

 ◄ Download the Cross Purposes One Colour Pattern UK Terms

 ◄ Download the Cross Purposes One Colour Pattern UK Terms with Left-handed charts

 ◄ Download the Cross Purposes One Colour Pattern US Terms

 ◄ Download the Cross Purposes One Colour Pattern US Terms with Left-handed charts

 ◄ Download the Cross Purposes Two Colour Pattern UK Terms

 ◄ Download the Cross Purposes Two Colour Pattern UK Terms with Left-handed charts

 ◄ Download the Cross Purposes Two Colour Pattern US Terms

 ◄ Download the Cross Purposes Two Colour Pattern US Terms with Left-handed charts

Cross Purposes Resources

Extending Cross Purposes

Repeat	Round	Side st count	Corners	Skip first st	Crosses	✓
	1	3	2-ch			
	2	5	2-ch	N		
	3	5	3-st	N		
	4	10	2-ch	N		
	5	14	2-ch		5	
	6	15	2-ch	Y		
	7	15	3-st	N		
	8	18	2-ch	Y		
1	9	22	2-ch		9	
	10	23	2-ch	Y		
	11	23	3-st	N		
	12	26	2-ch	Y		
2	13	30	2-ch		13	
	14	31	2-ch	Y		
	15	31	3-st	N		
	16	34	2-ch	Y		
3	17	38	2-ch		17	
	18	39	2-ch	Y		
	19	39	3-st	N		
	20	42	2-ch	Y		
4	21	46	2-ch		21	
	22	47	2-ch	Y		
	23	47	3-st	N		
	24	50	2-ch	Y		
5	25	54	2-ch		25	
	26	55	2-ch	Y		
	27	55	3-st	N		
	28	58	2-ch	Y		
6	29	62	2-ch		29	
	30	63	2-ch	Y		
	31	63	3-st	N		
	32	66	2-ch	Y		
7	33	70	2-ch		33	
	34	71	2-ch	Y		
	35	71	3-st	N		
	36	74	2-ch	Y		
8	37	78	2-ch		37	
	38	79	2-ch	Y		
	39	79	3-st	N		
	40	82	2-ch	Y		
9	41	86	2-ch		41	
	42	87	2-ch	Y		
	43	87	3-st	N		
	44	90	2-ch	Y		
10	45	94	2-ch		45	
	46	95	2-ch	Y		
	47	95	3-st	N		
	48	98	2-ch	Y		
11	49	102	2-ch		49	
	50	103	2-ch	Y		
	51	103	3-st	N		
	52	106	2-ch	Y		
12	53	110	2-ch		53	
	54	111	2-ch	Y		
	55	111	3-st	N		
	56	114	2-ch	Y		
13	57	118	2-ch		57	
	58	119	2-ch	Y		
	59	119	3-st	N		
	60	122	2-ch	Y		
14	61	126	2-ch		61	
	62	127	2-ch	Y		
	63	127	3-st	N		
	64	130	2-ch	Y		
15	65	134	2-ch		65	
	66	135	2-ch	Y		
	67	135	3-st	N		
	68	138	2-ch	Y		
16	69	142	2-ch		69	
	70	143	2-ch	Y		
	71	143	3-st	N		
	72	146	2-ch	Y		
17	73	150	2-ch		73	
	74	151	2-ch	Y		
	75	151	3-st	N		
	76	154	2-ch	Y		
18	77	158	2-ch		77	
	78	159	2-ch	Y		
	79	159	3-st	N		
	80	163	2-ch	Y		
19	81	166	2-ch		81	
	82	167	2-ch	Y		
	83	167	3-st	N		
	84	170	2-ch	Y		
20	85	174	2-ch		85	
	86	175	2-ch	Y		
	87	175	3-st	N		
	88	178	2-ch	Y		
21	89	182	2-ch		89	
	90	183	2-ch	Y		
	91	183	3-st	N		
	92	186	2-ch	Y		
22	93	190	2-ch		93	
	94	191	2-ch	Y		
	95	191	3-st	N		
	96	194	2-ch	Y		
23	97	198	2-ch		97	
	98	199	2-ch	Y		
	99	199	3-st	N		
	100	202	2-ch	Y		
24	101	206	2-ch		101	
	102	207	2-ch	Y		
	103	207	3-st	N		
	104	210	2-ch	Y		
25	105	214	2-ch		105	
	106	215	2-ch	Y		
	107	215	3-st	N		
	108	218	2-ch	Y		
26	109	222	2-ch		109	
	110	223	2-ch	Y		
	111	223	3-st	N		
	112	226	2-ch	Y		
27	113	230	2-ch		113	
	114	231	2-ch	Y		
	115	231	3-st	N		
	116	234	2-ch	Y		
28	117	238	2-ch		117	
	118	239	2-ch	Y		
	119	239	3-st	N		
	120	242	2-ch	Y		
29	121	246	2-ch		121	
	122	247	2-ch	Y		
	123	247	3-st	N		
	124	250	2-ch	Y		
30	125	254	2-ch		125	
	126	255	2-ch	Y		
	127	255	3-st	N		
	128*	258	2-ch	Y		

*Don't skip the first st of each side for the last repeat you do or if using as a border.

Brainstorming

Who is this for?

What do I want to make?

What yarn do I want to use? Colours?

Other WIPS?

Cross Purposes Resources

One Colour Project Planner

Yarn

Brand

Fibre

Weight

Colour

Total weight on hand

Hook

Size

Square size

Unblocked square size

Blocked square size

Blocking method used

Calculations

Weight of 1 square	(A)	
Number of squares needed	(B)	
Total weight for squares	(A x B = C)	
Joining and border	(10 to 20% of C = D)	
Total weight needed	(C + D = E)	

Two Colour Project Planner

Yarn

Brand
Fibre
Weight
Feature Colour
Main Colour
Total weight on hand -
      Feature Colour (FC)
      Main Colour (MC)

Hook

Size

Square size

Unblocked square size
Blocked square size
Blocking method used

Calculations

MC weight before making	(A)
MC weight after making	(B)
FC weight before making	(D)
FC weight after making	(E)
MC needed for 1 square	(A - B = C)
FC needed for 1 square	(D - E = F)
Number of squares needed	(G)
MC Total weight for squares	(C x G = H)
FC Total weight needed	(F x G = I)
MC Joining and border	(10 to 20% of H = J)
Total MC weight needed	(H + J = K)

Cross Purposes Resources

Layout Planner

One square: ____ cm/in   **Total project width:** ____ cm/in   **Total project length:** ____ cm/in

Thank You!

Well, there you have it.

I hope you have learned a lot you can transfer to other crochet projects.

Now, before I sign off, I want to thank some folks who helped make this happen.

Michelle Lorimer, as always, runs with my ideas and makes them work. And she has made Cross Purposes the fun, cool looking thing it is. Thank you, Michelle.

Thank you Leah Ladson, for capturing the Cross Purposes projects so well! You made them sing!

My testers were great! Simple as the Cross Purposes granny square pattern is, it went through a few iterations and my testing crew tried them all! Thank you Anne P, Melissa R, Michelle M, Ruth B, Teresa J, Stephanie B, and Ursula U.

Adele Pugh made the lovely scarf project for me, and I am ever so grateful for that. You'd still be waiting for this to be released if not for Adele. Thank you, Adele!

And a big thanks too, to Elizabeth Bell and Sarah Boyle raided their stashes for the samples you see in the planning your project lessons. It was so good to see my ideas come to life if your ways. Thank you!

Kelly Lonergan tech edited the patterns and checked the charts for me. Awesome meticulous work as always Kelly. Thank you!

And thank you! For your patience as I teased and teased, battling life and moving and travelling to get this done and for your enthusiasm for the project.

I hope you have enjoyed whatever parts you chose to do and keep on crocheting!

xx Shelley

About the Author

Shelley Husband is a designer, author, and serious supporter of making crocheting easy and enjoyable. While Shelley learned crocheting as a child, it took her almost 40 years to crochet her next granny square — and she hasn't stopped since.

Soon after that square, Shelley realised she had a new design in mind, and then another, and... well, let's just say, there's no slowing the new designs that continue to have her granny square community buzzing.

From her first book, Granny Square Flair, winning UK's Best Crochet Book in 2019, to this, her eleventh book, Shelley enjoys giving her community what they want. Now with an App, online group, and regular workshops across the country, Shelley loves getting the curious hooked on granny squares!

Old and new crocheters fall in love with the way Shelley designs patterns to be practical to grow their crochet confidence, one square at a time.

When Shelley's not running a retreat, working a workshop, or designing the next book from her hook, she's enjoying the lands of the Dja Dja Wurrung and the Taungurung Peoples of the Kulin Nation (also known as Bendigo in Victoria, Australia).

If you haven't joined her community already, and you are crochet curious, you're most welcome to look her up: **shelleyhusbandcrochet.com**.

Other Books by Shelley Husband

Granny Square Academy
Learn all there is to know about making granny squares, including how to read patterns.

Granny Square Academy 2
Expand your granny square knowledge with instructions for more advanced stitches and techniques.

Granny Square Flair
50 written and charted granny square patterns and 11 project ideas to make with them.

Beneath the Surface
A beginner friendly pattern, with lots of extra support including video links.

Siren's Atlas
64 written and charted granny square patterns for adventurous crocheters.

Granny Square Patchwork
40 written and charted granny square patterns of 6 sizes and 12 projects to make with them.

Dotty Spotty
Classic circle-to-square granny square fun.

Nimue Crochet Blanket
A crochet quest of epic proportions with very detailed help including video links.

The Cove
A pick your path pattern inspired by coastal adventures.

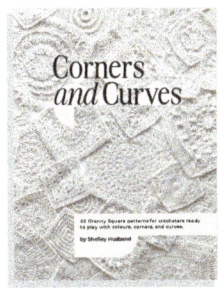

Corners and Curves
45 Granny squares for crocheters ready to play with colours, corners and curves.

Buy my books direct in my online shop or at most online book retailers around the world. Visit my pattern shop for digital patterns galore.

shop.shelleyhusbandcrochet.com

www.ingramcontent.com/pod-product-compliance
Lightning Source LLC
Chambersburg PA
CBHW061121070526
44583CB00028B/3353